LABORATORY MANUAL TO ACCOMPANY

Access Control, Authentication, and Public Key Infrastructure

JONES & BARTLETT
LEARNING

World Headquarters

Jones & Bartlett Learning
40 Tall Pine Drive
Sudbury, MA 01776
978-443-5000
info@jblearning.com
www.jblearning.com

Jones & Bartlett Learning Canada
6339 Ormindale Way
Mississauga, Ontario L5V 1J2
Canada

Jones & Bartlett Learning International
Barb House, Barb Mews
London W6 7PA
United Kingdom

Jones & Bartlett Learning books and products are available through most bookstores and online booksellers. To contact Jones & Bartlett Learning directly, call 800-832-0034, fax 978-443-8000, or visit our website, www.jblearning.com.

Substantial discounts on bulk quantities of Jones & Bartlett Learning publications are available to corporations, professional associations, and other qualified organizations. For details and specific discount information, contact the special sales department at Jones & Bartlett Learning via the above contact information or send an email to specialsales@jblearning.com.

Production Credits
Chief Executive Officer: Ty Field
President: James Homer
SVP, Chief Operating Officer: Don Jones, Jr.
SVP, Chief Technology Officer: Dean Fossella
SVP, Chief Marketing Officer: Alison M. Pendergast
SVP, Chief Financial Officer: Ruth Siporin
SVP, Curriculum Solutions: Christopher Will
VP, Design and Production: Anne Spencer
VP, Manufacturing and Inventory Control: Therese Connell
Author: vLab Solutions, LLC, David Kim, President
Editorial Management: Perspectives, Inc., Phil Graham, President
Reprints and Special Projects Manager: Susan Schultz
Associate Production Editor: Tina Chen
Director of Marketing: Alisha Weisman
Associate Marketing Manager: Meagan Norlund
Cover Design: Anne Spencer
Composition: vLab Solutions, LLC
Cover Image: © ErickN/ShutterStock, Inc.
Printing and Binding: Malloy, Inc.
Cover Printing: Malloy, Inc.

ISBN: 978-1-4496-1235-1

6048
Printed in the United States of America
14 13 12 11   10 9 8 7 6 5 4 3

Table of Contents

Current Version Date: 12/06/2010

Current Version Date: 12/06/2010

Current Version Date: 12/06/2010

ISS Curriculum Overview

The Bachelor of Science degree in Information Systems Security (ISS) is comprised of twelve foundational courses, each with ten (10) labs. The students will perform paper-based labs (design, configuration, or analysis) and hands-on labs using real equipment, security tools, and applications. The ISS curriculum is comprised of the following courses:

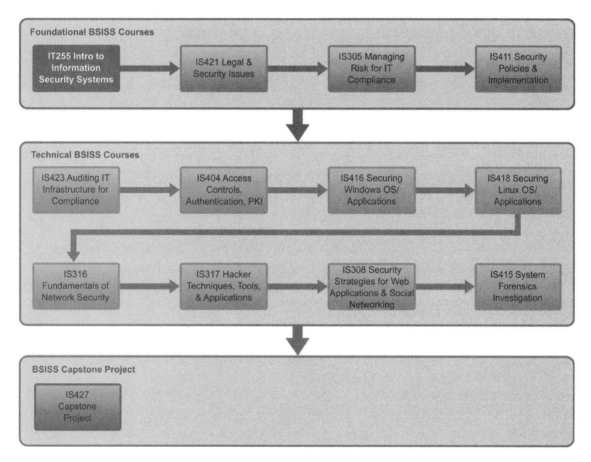

The introductory level courses, identified above in red, have paper-based labs with some accompanying hands-on labs. The security practitioner courses, in green above, have substantial hands-on lab exercises requiring students to be proficient with hardware, software, tools, and applications commonly found within the seven domains of a typical IT infrastructure.

The IS427 Capstone Project is the final course the ISS student takes prior to graduating from the program. This course encompasses all the accumulated knowledge obtained from the entire ISS curriculum, and it requires the student to respond to an RFP for information systems security consulting.

                                                                       Current Version Date: 12/06/2010

Ethics and Code of Conduct

Students enrolled in the ISS curriculum are aware that the hardware, software, tools, and applications presented and used within the ISS curriculum are for educational purposes only.

The students are not to use these tools, applications, or techniques on live production IT infrastructures. Under no circumstances shall they use these tools, applications, or techniques on ITT Technical Institute or the production IT infrastructures and networks of other organizations.

The students who are enrolled in the ISS curriculum are required to conform to ITT's Code of Conduct described in the student manual as well as the institution's general and specific policies.

Laboratory #1

Lab #1: Assess the Impact on Access Controls for a Regulatory Case Study

Learning Objectives and Outcomes

Upon completing this lab, students will be able to complete the following tasks:

1. Configure user accounts and access controls in a Windows Server according to role-based access implementation

2. Configure user account credentials as defined policy, and access right permissions for each user

3. Create and administer Group Policy Objects for the management of Windows Active Directory Domain machines within the IT infrastructure

4. Apply the correct Group Policy Object definitions per requirements defined by policies and access right permissions for users

5. Assign and manage access privileges as requested in the case study to apply the recommended and required security controls for the user accounts

Required Setup and Tools

This lab does not require the use of the ISS Mock IT Infrastructure - Cisco core backbone network. In addition, the Instructor VM workstation and Student VM workstations should be physically disconnected from the ITT internal network and be isolated on the classroom dedicated layer 2 switch. This will allow for a shared DHCP server to be used to allocate the IP addresses for the instructor and student workstations. The following equipment is required for this hands-on lab:

A) A classroom workstation (with at least 2 Gig RAM) capable of supporting the removable hard drive with the VM server farm connected to the classroom layer 2 switch.

B) An instructor workstation (with at least 4 Gig RAM recommended) that shall act as the Instructor's demo lab workstation. The instructor will display the Instructor workstation on the LCD projector to demo the loading and configuring of the Instructor VM workstation using VMware Player.

C) Students Lab workstations will use their own VM server farm and VM student workstation. VMware Player will be used to run the Student VM and the Target VM.

The following summarizes the setup, configuration, and equipment needed to perform Lab #1:

1. A Virtualized Server Farm with the following components:

Current Version Date: 12/06/2010

      a. Microsoft DHCP server for allocating student IP host addresses

      b. A Student and/or Instructor VM

      c. A Windows 2003 Server VM ("TargetWindows01")

2. Standard ITT onsite student workstation must have the following software applications loaded to perform this Lab:

      a. VMware Player 3.x

      b. Microsoft Office 2007 or higher for Lab Assessment Questions & Answers

Recommended Procedures

Hands-on Lab #1 – Student Steps:

Students should perform the following steps:

1. Connect the student-removable hard drive to your workstation

2. Boot up the student VM and Microsoft DHCP VM server to allocate an IP host address

3. Enable your DOS command prompt and type "ipconfig" and "ping" your allocated IP host address 172.30.0.___ , the DHCP server 172.30.0.10, and the IP default gateway router 172.30.0.1

4. Login to the Student VM using the following credentials:

Login ID: "student" (case sensitive)

Password: "ISS316Security" (case sensitive)

NOTE: If the workstations in your physical classroom have only 2GB of RAM then only two VMs can be powered-on at once. For this lab, you can load both the Student VM and the "TargetWindows01" Windows 2003 Server.

Create Active Directory Domain Objects

5. Power-on the "TargetWindows01" VM Server in VMware Player

6. Logon to the "TargetWindows01" VM Server.

- Windows Server 2003 Standard Edition 32-bit (VM Name: "TargetWindows01")
  - Computer Name: Windows02
  - Three Users Available: administrator, instructor, or student (case sensitive)
  - Password: ISS316Security (case sensitive)
  - IP Address: DHCP
  - Domain Login: NO

7. Upon login to the "TargetWindows01" VM Server, click Start > Run > and type into the DOS command prompt: dcpromo

Current Version Date: 12/06/2010

8. Answer all the necessary questions to create a New Active Directory Forest enabling DNS and reboot.

9. Log into "TargetWindows01" as an administrator of the new domain.

10. Create the following global domain user accounts and groups using Active Directory Users and Computers (Start -> Administrative Tools -> Active Directory Users and Computers):

    a. InspectorGeneral group

    b. FAR group

    c. SenateChairs group

    d. AwardedContracts group

    e. 'MBH1234' user account (use 'MBH!234pass' for the password) – member of InspectorGeneral group

    f. 'RJX-123' user account (use 'RJX-!23pass' for the password) – member of InspectorGeneral and AwardedContracts groups

    g. 'RXJ0123' user account (use 'RXJ0!23pass' for the password) – member of AwardedContracts group

    h. 'MBR0011' user account (use 'MBR00!!pass' for the password) – member of SenateChairs group

    i. The "Everyone" Group should be added as a member of the FAR group

11. Create the following four new folders:

    a. C:\FAR – This folder will contain miscellaneous shared files for the Federal Acquisition Regulation

    b. C:\FAR\SCfiles – Folder for shared Senate Chairs (SC) user files

    c. C:\FAR\IGfiles – Folder for shared Inspector General (IG) user files

    d. C:\FAR\ACfiles – Folder for shared Awarded Contracts (AC) user files

12. Determine what type of access controls are needed to allow the following actions:

    a. Allow Inspector General users to read and write files in C:\ FAR\IGfiles.

    b. Allow Senate Chairs users to read and write files in C:\ FAR\SCfiles.

    c. Allow Awarded Contracts users to read and write files in C:\ FAR\ACfiles and C:\ FAR\SCfiles.

Current Version Date: 12/06/2010

Create Group Policy Objects Definitions

13. Launch Active Directory Users and Computers on TargetWindows01: Start -> Administrative Tools -> Active Directory Users and Computers.

14. In the treeview, expand Forest -> Domains -> domainname -> right click Properties.

15. Select 'Group Policy Objects' open the context menu, (right-mouse-click on Group Policy Objects), select 'New'.

16. Create the following five new Domain Group Policies:

    a. Inspector General

    b. Federal Acquisition Regulation (FAR)

    c. Awarded Contracts

    d. Senate Chairs

    e. PasswordGPO

17. Open the context menu of the newly created PasswordGPO and select 'Edit...'.

18. In the Group Policy Management Editor treeview, expand Computer Configuration -> Policies -> Windows Settings -> Security Settings -> Account policies. Select 'Password Policy'.

19. Double-click 'Password must meet complexity requirements' and choose Enable. Choose 'OK'.

20. Double-click 'Minimum Password Length' and enter 8. Choose 'OK'.

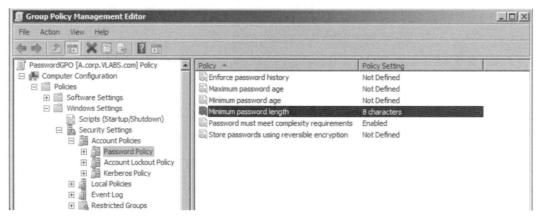

Figure 5 – Microsoft Windows Group Policy Management Editor

21. Close the Group Policy Management Editor.

22. Open the context menu for the domain and select 'Link an Existing GPO..."

23. Select 'PasswordGPO' and choose 'OK'.

www.jblearning.com

24. Then explain to the students that they are to "Link" each of the four other newly created GPOs to the Objects in Active Directory as defined in the following table (they will have to create and configure the files and settings as defined):

Group Policy Object	Files Created	User Assigned
Inspector General	*Annual audit*	*MBH1234* *RJX-123* *FAR*
	Closed Investigations	*Everyone*
	No Action Required	*Everyone*
Federal Acquisition Regulation (FAR)	*None*	*Everyone*
Awarded Contracts	*None*	*RXJ0123*
Senate Chairs	*Limited life*	*Senate Chairs* *MBR0011*

Figure 6 – User Access Control Requirements

Deliverables

Upon completion of Lab #1 - Assess the Impact on Access Controls for a Regulatory Case Study; students are required to provide the following deliverables:

1. Lab #1 – Group Policy Object Access /Control Requirements
2. Lab #1 – Lab Assessment Questions & Answers

Evaluation Criteria and Rubrics

The following are the evaluation criteria and rubrics for Lab #1 that the students must perform:

1. Was the student able to configure user accounts and access controls in a Windows Server according to role-based access implementation? – [**20%**]

2. Was the student able to configure user account credentials as per defined policy and access right permissions for each user? – [**20%**]

3. Was the student able to create and administer Group Policy Objects for the management of Windows Active Directory Domain machines within the IT infrastructure? – [**20%**]

4. Was the student able to apply the correct Group Policy Object definitions as per requirements defined by policies and access right permissions for users? – [**20%**]

5. Was the student able to assign and manage access privileges as requested in the case study to apply the recommended and required security controls for the user accounts? – [**20%**]

                                       Current Version Date: 12/06/2010

Lab #1 – Group Policy Object Assessment Worksheet

Course Name & Number: _____

Student Name: _____

Instructor Name: _____

Lab Due Date: _____

Overview

For this lab, the students must first define a Group Policy Object and the user access control requirements matrix. As part of this lab's deliverables, the students must submit screen captures of the user account configurations, user accounts associated with Group Policy objects, and permissions assigned to each user account.

Group Policy Object	Files Created	User Assigned

                                       Current Version Date: 12/06/2010

Lab #1 – Assessment Worksheet

Assess the Impact on Access Controls for a Regulatory Case Study

Course Name & Number: _____

Student Name: _____

Instructor Name: _____

Lab Due Date: _____

Overview

The students will create an Active Directory domain as well as user and group objects within the new domain. He/she will then create directories and assign permissions based on the required access control as defined in the matrix. Group Policy Objects will also be created and linked to Objects within the domain to enforce security settings.

Lab Assessment Questions & Answers

1. What does DACL stands for and what does it mean?

2. Why would you add permissions to a group instead of the individual?

3. List at least 3 different types of access control permissions available in Windows.

4. What are the least permissions that you need in order to view the contents of a folder?

5. What are other available Password Policy options that could be enforce to improve security?

6. Is using the option to 'Store passwords using reversible encryption' a good security practice? Why or why not? When should you enable the option to 'Store passwords using reversible encryption'?

7. What's the difference between a Local Group Policy and a Domain Group Policy?

8. In what order are all available Group Policies applied?

9. What is an Administrative Template as it refers to Windows Group Policy Objects?

10. What is the GPMC?

Current Version Date: 12/06/2010

Laboratory #2

Lab #2: Design Infrastructure Access Controls for a Network Diagram

Learning Objectives and Outcomes

Upon completing this lab, students will be able to complete the following tasks:

1. Identify where the security controls are needed within the seven domains of a typical IT infrastructure to ensure confidentiality, integrity, and availability (C-I-A) of information and system access

2. Specify what security access controls can mitigate the risk from unauthorized access throughout the seven domains of a typical IT infrastructure

3. Relate the impact of unauthorized access throughout the seven domains of a typical IT infrastructure for an organization

4. Apply the physical and logical access control solutions to assist with an overall layered security strategy throughout the seven domains of a typical IT infrastructure

5. Define the requirements for an access control policy definition that encompasses proper security controls throughout the seven domains of a typical IT infrastructure

Required Setup and Tools

This is a paper-based hands-on lab and does not require the use of the ISS "Mock" IT Infrastructure – Cisco core backbone network or VM server farm. Internet access and the student's Microsoft Office applications are needed to perform this hands-on paper-based lab.

The following summarizes the setup, configuration, and equipment needed to perform Lab #2:

1. Standard ITT ISS onsite student workstation must have the following software applications loaded and Internet access to perform this Lab:

    a. Microsoft Office 2007 or latest version

    b. Adobe PDF Reader

Recommended Procedures

Hands-on Lab #2 – Student Steps:

Students should perform the following steps:

1. Review the seven domains of a typical IT infrastructure with your students:

    a. User Domain

Current Version Date: 12/06/2010

      b.   Workstation Domain

      c.   Local Area Network (LAN) Domain

      d.   Local Area Network (LAN) – to – Wide Area Network (WAN) Domain

      e.   Wide Area Network (WAN) Domain

      f.   Remote Access Domain

      g.   Systems/Application Domain

2.   Have a general discussion about regarding the following question: "What if there were no access controls throughout the seven domains of a typical IT infrastructure?" – What would an attacker be able to do?

3.   Give examples of the access control security countermeasures throughout the seven domains of an IT infrastructure:

      a.   User Domain

          i.   Authentication Controls

         ii.   Security Employee Training and Awareness (SETA)

       iii.   Employee/Contractor background checks….

      b.   Workstation Domain

          i.   Host-based internal firewalls

         ii.   Anti-virus software and monitoring

       iii.   Patch management, etc…

      c.   Local Area Network (LAN) Domain

          i.   Firewalls

         ii.   Backup/Restore

       iii.   Monitoring, etc…

      d.   Local Area Network (LAN) to Wide Area Network (WAN) Domain

          i.   IDS/IPS

         ii.   DMZ

       iii.   Firewalls

       iv.   Traffic Monitoring

        v.   ACLs, etc…

      e.   Wide Area Network (WAN) Domain

          i.   Firewalls

         ii.   Traffic Monitoring

Current Version Date: 12/06/2010

           iii.   Content Monitoring, etc…

      f.   Remote Access Domain

           i.   Encryption, etc…

           ii.   IPSEC

           iii.   VPN through Internet

           iv.   SSL through Internet

           v.   Multi-factor Authentication

      g.   Systems/Application Domain

           i.   Role-based access controls

           ii.   Stringent file system and data access and permissions

           iii.   Multi-factor authentication

           iv.   Data and hard drive encryption

4. Discuss how these security countermeasures help achieve confidentiality, integrity and availability of information systems and data

5. Discuss how a layered approach throughout the seven domains of a typical IT infrastructure can help achieve access control policy definition and implementation goals

6. Complete the access controls design worksheet matrix and document requirements and access controls security countermeasures as part of a layered security strategy

Deliverables

Upon completion of Lab #2: Design Infrastructure Access Controls for a Network Diagram, students are required to provide the following deliverables:

1. Lab #2 – Access Controls Design Worksheet for Seven Domains of a Typical IT Infrastructure

2. Lab #2 – Lab Assessment Questions & Answers

Current Version Date: 12/06/2010

Evaluation Criteria and Rubrics

The following are the evaluation criteria and rubrics for Lab #2 that the students must perform:

1. Was the student able to identify where security controls are needed within the seven domains of a typical IT infrastructure to ensure confidentiality, integrity, and availability (C-I-A) of information and system access? – **[20%]**

2. Was the student able to specify what security access controls can mitigate the risk from unauthorized access throughout the seven domains of a typical IT infrastructure? – **[20%]**

3. Was the student able to relate the impact of unauthorized access throughout the seven domains of a typical IT infrastructure for an organization? – **[20%]**

4. Was the student able to apply physical and logical access control solutions to assist with an overall layered security strategy throughout the seven domains of a typical IT infrastructure? – **[20%]**

5. Was the student able to define the requirements for an access control policy that encompasses proper security controls throughout the seven domains of a typical IT infrastructure? – **[20%]**

                                                                   Current Version Date: 12/06/2010

Lab #2 – IT Domain Controls Assessment Worksheet

Design Infrastructure Access Controls for a Network Diagram

Course Name & Number: _____

Student Name: _____

Instructor Name: _____

Lab Due Date: _____

Overview

Fill in the following matrix with security controls to implement sound access controls throughout the seven domains of a typical IT infrastructure. Specify whether the security control achieves C-I-A and how it enhances security for that domain.

IT Domain	Controls to Implement within Domains	IT Asset or Entity Requiring Security Controls	Are Confidentiality, Integrity, and Availability Achieved?

Current Version Date: 12/06/2010

Lab #2 – Assessment Worksheet

Design Infrastructure Access Controls for a Network Diagram

Course Name & Number: _____

Student Name: _____

Instructor Name: _____

Lab Due Date: _____

Overview

In this lab the student conducts research on the controls related to the common IT domains and the implementation of controls to enhance information security (confidentiality, integrity and availability of information and information systems). The primary objectives to review for this lab are listed here:

- Review the seven domains of a typical IT infrastructure
- Identify how access controls can achieve confidentiality, integrity, and availability throughout a typical IT infrastructure
- Align risk exposure from unauthorized access to requirements for access controls
- Design layered physical and logical access controls

Lab Assessment Questions & Answers

1. Why is it important to perform a risk assessment on the systems, applications, and data prior to designing layered access controls?

2. What purpose does a Data Classification Standard have on designing layered access control systems?

3. You are tasked with creating a Microsoft Windows Enterprise Patch Management solution for an organization, but you have no budget. What options does Microsoft provide?

4. How does Monitoring the network and proper Incident Reporting help secure the infrastructure?

5. Provide an example of multi-factor authentication.

6. In what domain of a typical IT infrastructure would be the standard place to implement Anti-virus as a technical control? Explain.

                    Current Version Date: 12/06/2010

7. What is the difference between a Host-based Firewall and a Network-based Firewall? What domains would you deploy each of these? Explain.

8. Give at least 3 examples of Controls typically implemented in the User Domain. Explain these controls.

9. Provide 3 examples of encrypted remote access communications (i.e., remote access via Internet).

10. Which domain within a typical IT infrastructure is the weakest link in the entire IT infrastructure?

Current Version Date: 12/06/2010

Laboratory #3

Lab #3: Identify & Classify Data for Access Control Requirements

Learning Objectives and Outcomes

Upon completing this lab, students will be able to complete the following tasks:

- Identify the impact that unauthorized access and security breaches have on both private sector and public sector organizations

- Define an organization-wide authorization and access policy for all types of data used throughout the IT infrastructure's systems, applications, and data

- Align an organizational authorization and access policy to accommodate the requirements of a data classification standard

- Develop a plan to classify data and implement proper security controls based on the data classification to ensure privacy and confidentiality

- Define an access control policy framework that defines the proper implementation for access throughout the seven domains of a typical IT infrastructure

Required Setup and Tools

This lab does not require the use of the ISS Mock IT Infrastructure - Cisco core backbone network. In addition, the Instructor VM workstation and Student VM workstations should be physically disconnected from the ITT internal network and be isolated on the classroom dedicated layer 2 switch. This will allow for a shared DHCP server to be used to allocate the IP addresses for the instructor and student workstations. The following is required for this hands-on lab:

A) A classroom workstation (with at least 2 Gig RAM) capable of supporting the removable hard drive with the VM server farm connected to the classroom layer 2 switch.

B) An instructor workstation (with at least 4 Gig RAM recommended) that shall act as the Instructor's demo lab workstation. The instructor will display the Instructor workstation on the LCD projector to demo the loading and configuring of the Instructor VM workstation using VMware Player.

C) Students Lab workstations will use their own VM server farm and VM student workstation. VMware Player will be used to run the Student VM and the Target VM.

Current Version Date: 12/06/2010

The following summarizes the setup, configuration, and equipment needed to perform Lab #3:

1. A Virtualized Server Farm with the following components:

    a. Microsoft DHCP server for allocating student IP host addresses

    b. A Student and/or Instructor VM workstation

    c. A Windows 2003 Server VM ("TargetWindows01")

2. Standard ITT onsite student workstation must have the following software applications loaded to conduct this Lab:

    a. VMware Player 3.x

    b. Microsoft Office 2007 or higher for Lab Assessment Questions & Answers

Recommended Procedures

Hands-on Lab #3 – Student Steps:

Students should perform the following steps:

1. Connect the student-removable hard drive to your workstation

2. Boot up the student VM and Microsoft DHCP VM server to allocate an IP host address

3. Enable your DOS command prompt and type "ipconfig" and "ping" your allocated IP host address 172.30.0.__ , the DHCP server 172.30.0.10, and the IP default gateway router 172.30.0.1

4. Login to the Student VM using the following credentials:

    Login ID: "student" (case sensitive)

    Password: "ISS316Security" (case sensitive)

NOTE: If the workstations in your physical classroom have only 2GB of RAM then only two VMs can be powered-on at once. For this lab, you can load both the Student VM and the "TargetWindows01" Windows 2003 Server.

---

5. Review the Data Classification Scheme provided.

                                                       Current Version Date: 12/06/2010

Table 1: Data Classification Scheme

Data Classification Scheme		
Classification	**Potential Impact**	**Example Data Types**
Public	➢ None or limited ➢ mention in local media; ➢ no impact on operations, financial performance or public image	Published documents, web pages, newspaper advertisements, non-sensitive, information
Internal Use Only	Limited impact from negative publicity, ➢ slight image or financial harm not prolonged or severe in nature	Internal memorandums of operations, continuing contracts, private customer information, short-term operating results and strategy
Confidential	More severe that Limited ➢ impact from negative publicity up to 6 months ➢ moderate image or financial harm < $5 million over 6 – 12 months	Critical and sensitive operating reports, personnel records, pay records, medical records, severe workforce management information, Periodic financial information reported to the public
Restricted	Severe impairment to public image and financial operations ➢ Impairs customer and public trust ➢ >$10 million loss in 3 months ➢ Sustained negative publicity expected for 1 or more years ➢ Impairs ability to execute operation and strategic 3 – 5 years in development and execution.	Strategic plans, communications with the board of directors or with Joint Venture boards of directors, Internal investigations, strategic expansion plans and associated workforce management,

Current Version Date: 12/06/2010

6. Review the Job Roles and Network Connectivity Modes provided.

Table 2: Job Roles and Network Connectivity mode

Acme Incorporated	
Individual Organization Roles	Network Connectivity
➢ CEO – Chief Executive Officer	Workstation, mobile pc and iPhone
➢ Remote Plant Manager	Workstation via remote access
➢ SW Area General Mgr	Workstation – network connected
➢ SVP International Acquisitions	mobile pc and iPhone
➢ Executive VP HR	Workstation, mobile pc and iPhone
➢ EVP Marketing	Workstation, mobile pc and iPhone
➢ SW Store Manager	Workstation
➢ NWR Store Sales Clerk	Cash register - network access for downloads
➢ NWR Receiving Clerk	RF for inventory management
➢ Public Customer	Internet only
➢ Online Customer	Internet
➢ Corporate Controller	Workstation, mobile pc and iPhone
➢ Information Security Specialist	Workstation, mobile pc and iPhone

7. Power-on the "TargetWindows01" VM Server in VMware Player

8. Logon to the "TargetWindows01" VM Server using "administrator"

- Windows Server 2003 Standard Edition 32-bit (VM Name: "TargetWindows01")
  o Computer Name: Windows02
  o Three Users Available: administrator, instructor, or student (case sensitive)
  o Password: ISS316Security (case sensitive)
  o IP Address: DHCP
  o Domain Login: NO

9. Create Users, Groups and GPOs as defined in Table 1 and Table 2 above

10. Manage properties/security of the groups and add users accounts

Deliverables

Upon completion of Lab #3: Identify & Classify Data for Access Control Requirements, students are required to provide the following deliverables:

1. Lab #3 – Data Classification Matrix Assessment Worksheet
2. Lab #3 – Assessment Worksheet with answers to the assessment questions

Evaluation Criteria and Rubrics

The following are the evaluation criteria and rubrics for Lab #3 that the students must perform:

1. Was the student able to identify the impacts that unauthorized access and security breaches have on both private sector and public sector organizations? – [**20%**]

2. Was the student able to define an organization-wide authorization and access policy for all types of data used throughout the IT infrastructure's systems, applications, and data? – [**20%**]

3. Was the student able to align an organizational authorization and access policy to accommodate the requirements of a data classification standard? – [**20%**]

4. Was the student able to develop a plan to classify data and implement proper security controls based on the data classification to ensure privacy and confidentiality? – [**20%**]

5. Was the student able to define an access control policy framework that defines the proper implementation for access throughout the seven domains of a typical IT infrastructure? – [**20%**]

Current Version Date: 12/06/2010

Lab #3 – Data Classification Matrix Assessment Worksheet

Course Name & Number: _____

Student Name: _____

Instructor Name: _____

Lab Due Date: _____

Overview

In this lab, the student is required to fill out the Data Classification Matrix based on the information provided in Table 1 and Table 2 of this lab. In the Data Classification Matrix following, classify the data by inserting an "X" in the column. Each data item can have only classification. Then decide the roles that should have access to the data based on job function listed.

Data Classification Matrix

Acme Incorporated					
Data/Information Classification Matrix					
Document to Classify	**Public**	**Internal Use Only**	**Confidential**	**Restricted**	**Who Should Have Access**
Monthly Terminations and new hire report					
Contract for long term lease of in Singapore					
NWR receiving report					
China sales forecast with projected revenue based on 3 year expansion plan					
NWR Sales results by product category					

                                                         Current Version Date: 12/06/2010

Acme Incorporated					
Data/Information Classification Matrix					
Document to Classify	**Public**	**Internal Use Only**	**Confidential**	**Restricted**	**Who Should Have Access**
Community involvement information published on Corporate Intranet released by Public Affairs					
NWR manpower workforce reduction					
SW Weekly store operating results					
Strategic planning documents for changing core organizational functions					
Online product catalog					
Executive reports to the Board of Directors					
Internal fraud investigation from SW region involving the SW Area General Manager					
Report of a minor <$50 credit card fraud perpetrated by a customer at a Eastern store					

Lab #3 – Assessment Worksheet

Identify & Classify Data for Access Control Requirements

Course Name & Number: _____

Student Name: _____

Instructor Name: _____

Lab Due Date: _____

Overview

This lab provides the student with the opportunity to develop data classification guidelines and to classify data access based on the job responsibilities – not an organizational position. He/she will have the opportunity to develop and deploy classification standards and the access controls necessary to ensure confidentiality, integrity and availability of information and information systems. Answer the following assessment questions.

Lab Assessment Questions & Answers

1. What is the Data Classification Method used in the Military and Government Agencies that line up with the corporate data classification method defined earlier in this lab? Explain.

2. Describe one way to help prevent unauthorized users from logging onto another person's user account and accessing his/her data?

3. What permissions are necessary to allow an Active Directory Group called AD_Group to read and write files in a Sensitive directory such as C:\ERPdocuments\HRfiles?

4. How would you apply the permissions (ACLs) stated above (M,RX) to the AD_Group on C:\ERPdocuments\HRfiles *from the command prompt* using built-in Windows tools?

5. When adding permissions to a directory in an Active Directory Domain, would you prefer to add Groups or individual User accounts to said directories? Explain.

Current Version Date: 12/06/2010

6. Based on Microsoft's Step-by-Step Guide on Understanding GPOs http://technet.microsoft.com/en-us/library/bb742376.aspx what is the significance of the "Block Inheritance" feature of GPOs and why would it be used?

7. What is the importance of the Security Groups created and why would we setup Security Group Filtering for GPOs as we have done?

8. Explain the Principle of Least Privilege.

9. How does a Data Classification Standard influence your access control strategy?

10. List and explain at least 3 benefits derived from properly implementing the Principle of Least Privilege

Current Version Date: 12/06/2010

-29-

Laboratory #4

Lab #4: Implement Organizational-Wide Network and WLAN Access Controls

Learning Objectives and Outcomes

Upon completing this Lab, students will be able to complete the following tasks:

- Review a case study on the access control policies and data classification standard of an organization
- Assess the impact that unauthorized access and security breaches have on both private sector and public sector organizations
- Configure the internal firewall for Microsoft Windows 2003 Server and Windows XP Workstation based on a policy definition
- Draft a WLAN security implementation plan to address confidentiality, integrity, and availability of WLAN services
- Develop an implementation plan regarding the proper deployment of organization-wide access controls throughout the seven domains of a typical IT infrastructure

Required Setup and Tools

This lab does not require the use of the ISS Mock IT Infrastructure - Cisco core backbone network. In addition, the Instructor VM workstation and Student VM workstations should be physically disconnected from the ITT internal network and be isolated on the classroom dedicated layer 2 switch. This will allow for a shared DHCP server to be used to allocate the IP addresses for the instructor and student workstations. The following is required for this hands-on lab:

A) A classroom workstation (with at least 2 Gig RAM) capable of supporting the removable hard drive with the VM server farm connected to the classroom layer 2 switch.

B) An instructor workstation (with at least 4 Gig RAM recommended) that will act as the Instructor's demo lab workstation. He/she will display the Instructor workstation on the LCD projector to demo the loading and configuring of the Instructor VM workstation using VMware Player.

C) Student Lab workstations will use their own VM server farm and VM student workstation. VMware Player will be used to run the Student VM and the Target VM.

Current Version Date: 12/06/2010

The following summarizes the setup, configuration, and equipment needed to perform Lab #4:

1. A Virtualized Server Farm with the following components:

    a. Microsoft DHCP server for allocating student IP host addresses

    b. A Student and/or Instructor VM workstation

    c. A Windows 2003 Server VM (TargetWindows01)

2. Standard ITT ISS onsite student workstation must have the following software applications loaded to perform this Lab:

    a. VMware Player 3.x

    b. Microsoft Office 2007 or higher for Lab Assessment Questions & Answers

Recommended Procedures

Hands-on Lab #4 – Student Steps:

Students should perform the following steps:

1. Connect the instructor removable hard drive to your workstation

2. Boot up the instructor VM and Microsoft DHCP VM server to allocate an IP host address

3. Enable your DOS command prompt and type "ipconfig" and "ping" your allocated IP host address 172.30.0.__ , the DHCP server 172.30.0.10, and the IP default gateway router 172.30.0.1

4. Login to the Instructor VM using the following credentials:

    Login ID: "instructor" (case sensitive)

    Password: "ISS316Security" (case sensitive)

NOTE: If the workstations in your physical classroom have only 2GB of RAM then only two VMs can be powered-on at once. For this lab, you can load both the Instructor VM and the "TargetWindows01" Windows 2003 Server. The DHCP server must be enabled on a different workstation connected to the classroom layer 2 switch.

---

5. Power-on the "TargetWindows01" and "WindowsDHCP01" VM Server in VMware Player

6. Logon to the "TargetWindows01" VM Server using "administrator"

    - Windows Server 2003 Standard Edition 32-bit (VM Name: "TargetWindows01")
      o   Computer Name: Windows02
      o   Three Users Available: administrator, instructor, or student (case sensitive)
      o   Password: ISS316Security (case sensitive)
      o   IP Address: DHCP
      o   Domain Login: NO

Current Version Date: 12/06/2010

7. Perform a demonstration of a successful PING, as well as a TFTP, and FTP file transfer to demonstrate the default settings of a Windows internal firewall if enabled

8. Configure the host-based firewall based on the following organizational policy:

   • Implement the default Microsoft Windows internal firewall

   • Add/Block the following additional programs:

     - Yahoo Messenger IM Chat

   • Block the following applications:

     - TELNET
     - TFTP
     - SNMP
     - ICMP echo-request
     - ICMP echo-reply

   • Allow the following applications under ADVANCED settings:

     - FTP
     - SMTP
     - POP3
     - HTTPS
     - HTTP

9. Load and run Windows Security Center from the Control Panel of the Target Windows01 server

10. Click and run Windows Firewall and demo the settings and configuration parameters listed under GENERAL, EXCEPTIONS, and ADVANCED

11. Display the DEFAULT settings for Windows Firewall

12. Demo how to enable exception rules and advanced settings such as port number filtering

13. Configure PING, TELNET and TFTP traffic to be denied using the internal firewall

14. Perform a validation test to verify that the exception rules and advanced settings work properly by attempting to connect from Instructor VM to Target VM once again:

    • Test and verify PING does not work.

    • Test and verify TFTP does not work

    • Test and verify TFTP does not work

    • Test and verify HTTP does work

    • Test and verify FTP does work

Current Version Date: 12/06/2010

WLAN Research Portion

15. Download the and review the IASE documents provided by DISA for DoD regarding Wireless Security: http://iase.disa.mil/stigs/downloads/zip/unclassified_wireless_stig_v6r2_20100423.zip

16. Extract the zip file, then open and review the U_Wireless_STIG_ V6R2_Final_20100423.pdf document

17. Discuss section on "How to Perform a Wireless Review"

18. Sample Interview Questions

19. Wireless Process Matrix

20. Discuss WLAN Compliance Requirements

21. Discuss WLAN Network Devices

22. Discuss WLAN Clients

23. Discuss PDA, Cell-phones and Non-wireless E-mail device Compliance Requirements

Deliverables

Upon completion of Lab #4: Implement Organizational-Wide Access Controls, students are required to provide the following deliverables:

1. Lab #4 – ACL and WLAN Assessment Worksheet: Use the tables to correctly and effectively respond to the wireless and network security questions. With the completed table submit screen image prints/captures to show configuration is effective and implemented.

2. Lab #4 – Assessment Worksheet with answers to the assessment questions

Evaluation Criteria and Rubrics

The following are the evaluation criteria and rubrics for Lab #4 that the students must perform:

1. Review a case study on the access control policies and data classification standard of an organization

2. Assess the impact that unauthorized access and security breaches have on both private sector and public sector organizations

3. Configure the internal firewall for Microsoft Windows 2003 Server and Windows XP Workstation based on a policy definition

4. Draft a WLAN security implementation plan to address confidentiality, integrity, and availability of WLAN services

5. Develop an implementation plan regarding the proper deployment of organization-wide access controls throughout the seven domains of a typical IT infrastructure

Current Version Date: 12/06/2010

Lab #4 – ACL and Windows Firewall Assessment Worksheet

Course Name & Number: _____

Student Name: _____

Instructor Name: _____

Lab Due Date: _____

Overview

Review the default settings for your Windows internal host-based firewall and indicate what you would recommend.

Access Control Lists (ACLs) and Firewall Design Worksheet:

GENERAL

_____ – Recommended (Firewall On/Off)

_____ – Don't Allow Exception Rules (On/Off)

_____ – Not Recommended (On/Off)

EXCEPTIONS

_____ – File Print Sharing

_____ – Remote Assistance

_____ – Remote Desktop

_____ - uPnP Framework

ADVANCED

_____ – Network Connection Settings

          _____ - 1394 Connections

          _____ - Cisco AnyConnect VPN

          _____ - Local Area Connection

          _____ - Wireless Network Connection

_____ – Security Logging

          _____ - Logging Options

          _____ - Logging File Options

                                                     Current Version Date: 12/06/2010

_____ – ICMP

     _____ - Allow incoming request

     _____ - Allow incoming time request

     _____ - Allow incoming router request

     _____ - Allow outgoing destination unreachable

     _____ - Allow outgoing source quench

     _____ - Allow outgoing parameter problem

     _____ - Allow outgoing time exceeded

     _____ - Allow redirect

     _____ - Allow outgoing packet too big

Current Version Date: 12/06/2010

Lab #4 – Assessment Worksheet

Implement Organizational-Wide Network and WLAN Access Controls

Course Name & Number: _____

Student Name: _____

Instructor Name: _____

Lab Due Date: _____

Overview

In this lab, the students enable and configure their internal host-based Windows workstation firewall. They use their own Student VM and Target VMs to test their own internal host-based firewall configurations. They also performWireless LAN research and review Wireless LAN (WLAN) security standards from NIST and IASE documents.

Lab Assessment Questions & Answers

1. What risk exposure are you subjecting your Microsoft Windows systems to by opening up ports on your internal firewall?

2. Using the VM's on your student workstation, how can you test if your Windows internal firewall is configured properly?

3. Name at least three significant risks of logging in to access points in airports, hotels and other public places? Explain.

4. Name at least three WLAN network devices commonly found in enterprise WLAN systems.

5. Name at least 5 methods of wireless communications that need to be secured and accounted for in a typical enterprise environment?

6. How does Bluetooth communication differ from a regular WLAN with access points and clients?

7. What are the risks involved in having the wired and wireless NICs enabled simultaneously on a laptop or workstation?

Current Version Date: 12/06/2010

8. What is the major reason why WEP encryption is not suitable for securing a WLAN connection? What is recommended for use with WLAN infrastructures?

9. What is a Man-in-the-Middle Attack? Explain.

10. What is a Network Injection Attack? Explain.

Current Version Date: 12/06/2010

Laboratory #5

Lab #5: Enhance Security Controls for Access to Sensitive Data

Learning Objectives and Outcomes

Upon completing this lab, students will be able to complete the following tasks:

- Define proper access controls for employees, contractors, and third-parties in accordance with defined access control policy definition

- Identify best practices for conducting interviews and background checks to mitigate the risk within the User Domain

- Describe best practices regarding hiring, job rotations, and separation of duties to mitigate the risk within the User Domain

- Apply best practices within acceptable use policies and confidentiality agreements to mitigate the risk within the User Domain

- Implement best practices for minimizing employee exposure to sensitive data such as employee security awareness training, encryption, or sanitization of data where appropriate

Required Setup and Tools

This is a paper-based hands-on lab and does not require the use of the ISS "Mock" IT Infrastructure – Cisco core backbone network or VM server farm. Internet access and the student's Microsoft Office applications are needed to perform this hands-on paper-based lab.

The following summarizes the setup, configuration, and equipment needed to perform Lab #5:

1. Standard ITT ISS onsite student workstation must have the following software applications loaded and Internet access to perform this Lab:

    a. Microsoft Office 2007 or higher

    b. Adobe PDF Reader

Recommended Procedures

Hands-on Lab #5 – Student Steps

Students should perform the following steps:

1. Download and review the DoD document provided by IASE for DISA called Access Control in Support of Information Systems:

    http://iase.disa.mil/stigs/stig/access_control_stig_v2r2_final_26_dec_2008.pdf

                                   Current Version Date: 12/06/2010

2. Investigate the following Access Control Layers:

    a. The Access Control Perimeter

    b. Asset Containers

    c. Workplace Perimeter

3. Investigate Access Control Methods and Technical Strategies

    a. Identification, Authentication and Authorization

    b. Logical Access Controls

        i.   Network Architecture Controls

        ii.   Remote Network Access

        iii. Security Network Ports

        iv.   Encryption

        v.   PKI Compliance Requirements

        vi.   Passwords, PINs, and Implementations of "Something You Know"

    c. Physical Access Controls

        i.   Classified Storage and Handling

        ii.   Badges, Memory Cards and Smart Cards

        iii. Physical Tokens and Physical Intrusion Detection Systems

4. Investigate the following Access Control Integration and Administrative Strategies:

    a. Biometric Systems

    b. Separation of Duties

    c. Protecting the Enrollment Process

    d. Protecting the Verification Process

    e. Cryptographic Controls

    f. Risk Analysis

    g. Integrating Access Control Methods

5. Investigate the following Key Infrastructure (PKI):

    a. DoD Approved PKI

    b. Multi-factor Authentication

    c. Identification and authentication through digital signature of a challenge

    d. Data integrity through digital signature of the information

    e. Confidentiality through encryption

    f. Assists with technical non-repudiation through digital signatures

6. Investigate these concepts on mitigating risk in the User Domain:

    a. Interviewing and background screening

    b. Hiring, job rotations, and separation of duties

    c. Security Policies

7. Discuss how to implement the following:

    a. Acceptable Use Policies

    b. Confidentiality Agreements

    c. Non-compete agreements

    d. Best practices for minimizing employee exposure to sensitive data

    e. New employee orientation training

    f. On-going Security Awareness training

Deliverables

Upon completion of Lab #5: Enhance Security Controls for Access to Sensitive Data, students are required to provide the following deliverables:

1. Lab #5 – Develop a chart listing at least 5 Technical Controls and 5 Administrative Controls that are required for properly implementing access control in the User Domain. Include a description of the controls for each after the chart, explaining why, in your opinion, these are the most valuable controls with which to start. Please keep this report under 500 words.

2. Lab #5 – Lab Assessment Questions & Answers

www.jblearning.com
Current Version Date: 12/06/2010

Evaluation Criteria and Rubrics

The following are the evaluation criteria and rubrics for Lab #5 that the students must perform:

1. Was the student able to define proper access controls for employees, contractors, and third-parties in accordance with defined access control policy definition? – [**20%**]

2. Was the student able to identify best practices for performing interviews and background checks to mitigate the risk within the User Domain? – [**20%**]

3. Was the student able to describe best practices regarding hiring, job rotations, and separation of duties to mitigate the risk within the User Domain? – [**20%**]

4. Was the student able to apply best practices within acceptable use policies and confidentiality agreements to mitigate the risk within the User Domain? – [**20%**]

5. Was the student able to implement best practices for minimizing employee exposure to sensitive data such as employee security awareness training, encryption, or sanitization of data where appropriate? – [**20%**]

Lab #5 – Assessment Worksheet

Enhance Security Controls for Access to Sensitive Data

Course Name & Number: _____

Student Name: _____

Instructor Name: _____

Lab Due Date: _____

Overview

The student will enhance security controls by controlling access to sensitive data and reviewing best practices for maintain security in the User Domain. To do this, he/she will download a Best Practices document called a STIG from the DoD website provided by IASE a division of DISA. The Access Control document reviews all the possible logical and physical controls required to properly secure and classify data through identification, authentication and authorization. The student will develop a chart listing at least 5 Technical Controls and 5 Administrative Controls that are required for properly implementing access control in the User Domain. Include a description of how each security control mitigates the risk exposure within the User Domain.

Lab Assessment Questions & Answers

1. What are the three major categories used to provide authentication of an individual?

2. What is Authorization and how is this concept aligned with Identification and Authentication?

3. Provide at least 3 examples of Network Architecture Controls that help enforce data access policies at the LAN-to-WAN Domain level?

4. When a computer is physically connected to a network port, manual procedures and/or an automated method must exist to perform what type of security functions at the Network Port and Data Switch level for access control? Name and define at least three.

5. What is a Network Access Control (NAC) System? Explain its benefits in securing access control to a network.

Current Version Date: 12/06/2010

6. Explain the purpose of a Public Key Infrastructure (PKI) and give an example of how you would implement it in a large organization whose major concern is the proper distribution of certificates across many sites.

7. PKI provides the capabilities of digital signatures and encryption to implement what security services? Name at least three.

8. What is the X.509 standard and how does it relate to PKI?

9. What is the difference between Identification and Verification in regard to Biometric Access Controls?

10. Provide a written explanation of what implementing Separation of Duties would look like in regard to managing a PKI Infrastructure for a large organization.

Current Version Date: 12/06/2010

Laboratory #6

Lab #6: Enhance Security Controls Leveraging Group Policy Objects

Learning Objectives and Outcomes

Upon completing this lab, the students will be able to complete the following tasks:

- Define layered access control lists for file system access based on users, groups and applications required based on roles and Group Policy Objects

- Apply User Rights Assignments to Group Policy Objects enforcing time zones, application restrictions, backup and encryption options

- Align proper access controls for the three states of data within an information system by aligning read-write-delete access rights to different file types as per data owner permission requirements

- Define appropriate access control rights for end-users, system administrators, and super-user account privileges based on a data classification standard

- Implement access control best practices for Windows Active Directory and user access control features for Windows servers and workstation

Required Setup and Tools

This lab does not require the use of the ISS Mock IT Infrastructure - Cisco core backbone network. In addition, the Instructor VM workstation and Student VM workstations should be physically disconnected from the ITT internal network and be isolated on the classroom dedicated layer 2 switch. This will allow for a shared DHCP server to be used to allocate the IP addresses for the instructor and student workstations. The following components are required for this hands-on lab:

A) A classroom workstation (with at least 2 Gig RAM) capable of supporting the removable hard drive with the VM server farm connected to the classroom layer 2 switch.

B) An instructor workstation (with at least 4 Gig RAM recommended) that shall act as the Instructor's demo lab workstation. The instructor will display the Instructor workstation on the LCD projector to demo the loading and configuring of the Instructor VM workstation using VMware Player.

C) Students will use their own VM server farm and VM student workstation. VMware Player will be used to run the Student VM and the Target VM.

-44-

The following summarizes the setup, configuration, and equipment needed to perform Lab #6:

1. A Virtualized Server Farm with these components:

    a. Microsoft DHCP server for allocating student IP host addresses

    b. A Student and/or Instructor VM workstation

    c. A Windows 2003 Server VM ("TargetWindows01")

2. Standard ITT ISS onsite student workstation must have the following software applications

    loaded to perform this Lab:

    a. VMware Player 3.x

    b. Microsoft Office 2007 or higher for Lab Assessment Questions & Answers

Recommended Procedures

Hands-on Lab #6 – Student Steps:

Students should perform the following steps:

1. Connect the student-removable hard drive to your workstation

2. Boot up the student VM and Microsoft DHCP VM server to allocate an IP host address

3. Enable your DOS command prompt and type "ipconfig" and "ping" your allocated IP host

    address 172.30.0.__ , the DHCP server 172.30.0.10, and the IP default gateway router 172.30.0.1

4. Login to the Student VM using the following credentials:

    Login ID: "student" (case sensitive)

    Password: "ISS316Security" (case sensitive)

NOTE: If the workstations in your physical classroom have only 2GB of RAM then only two VMs can

be powered-on at once. For this lab, you can load both the Student VM and the "TargetWindows01"

Windows 2003 Server.

---

5. Login to the "TargetWindows01" VM server:

    ▪ Windows Server 2003 Standard Edition 32-bit (VM Name: "TargetWindows01")
        o Computer Name: Windows02
        o Three Users Available: administrator, instructor, or student (case sensitive)
        o Password: ISS316Security (case sensitive)
        o IP Address: DHCP
        o Domain Login: NO

6. Launch Active Directory Users and Computers on TargetWindows01: Start -> Administrative

    Tools -> Active Directory Users and Computers.

7. In the tree view, expand Forest -> Domains -> domainname -> right click Properties.

8. Select 'Group Policy Objects' open the context menu, (right-mouse-click on Group Policy Objects).

9. Use the GPOs created in Lab 1 to customize and add User Rights Assignment to the following four GPOs:

    a. Inspector General

    b. Federal Acquisition Regulation (FAR)

    c. Awarded Contracts

    d. Senate Chairs

10. Ensure that the assigned users are part of its corresponding groups and GPO

11. Find User Rights Assignments under Policies on each of the GPOs

12. Assign at least one group appropriate application restriction to each GPO

13. Users should have appropriate access rights and permissions to the data they require

14. Provide remote access considerations provided for Senate Chairs and Inspector General Users

15. Consider/implement the access time restrictions considered for users and international locations for the Senate Chairs group members

16. Give/provide considerations for backup and recovery for all groups

17. Show a screenshot of what policies you would set if you were to consider encryption on some/all of the file systems

18. Build a matrix to identify the common needs of each data file, application and user and provide it as feedback

19. Build GPOs to group access and rights requirements

20. Provide a detail description and screenshot of the User Rights Assignments and Policy Settings chosen for each of the four GPOs

Deliverables

Upon completion of Lab #6: Enhance Security Controls Leveraging Group Policy Objects, students are required to provide the following deliverables:

1. Lab #6 –Lab deliverables include screen captures of the GPO's and user rights settings implemented in the hands-on lab

2. Lab #6 – Lab Assessment Questions & Answers

Current Version Date: 12/06/2010

Evaluation Criteria and Rubrics

The following are the evaluation criteria and rubrics for Lab #6 that the students must perform:

- Was the student able to define layered access control lists for file system access based on users, groups and applications required based on roles and Group Policy Objects? – [**20%**]

- Was the student able to apply User Rights Assignments to Group Policy Objects enforcing time zones, application restrictions, backup and encryption options? – [**20%**]

- Was the student able to align proper access controls for the three states of data within an information system by aligning read-write-delete access rights to different file types as per data owner permission requirements? – [**20%**]

- Was the student able to define appropriate access control rights for end-users, system administrators, and super-user account privileges based on a data classification standard? – [**20%**]

- Was the student able to implement access control best practices for Windows Active Directory and user access control features for Windows servers and workstation? – [**20%**]

Current Version Date: 12/06/2010

Lab #6 – Assessment Worksheet

Enhance Security Controls Leveraging Group Policy Objects

Course Name & Number: _____

Student Name: _____

Instructor Name: _____

Lab Due Date: _____

Overview

This lab is an extension of Lab #1 and includes additional security access controls that can be enabled within Applications and Groups in the created Group Policy Objects. Using the user accounts and group definitions created in Lab #1, the students will apply user rights based on user group definitions and GPOs. They will also define encryption options, data backup and recovery strategies necessary to enhance the security controls defined by policy statements. They will also configure the access controls and restrictions to accommodate users from different time zones and international users.

Lab Assessment Questions & Answers

1. What are the available Password Policy options that could be enforced to improve security in a Group Policy Object?

2. How would you set security permissions and user access rights on a home computer using Windows XP Professional or similar that is not a member of the domain?

3. Why is the use of the different password policy options available, and why is it important to implement complexity and length requirements?

4. Microsoft defines user rights in two types of categories: Logon Rights and Privileges. Explain the difference of the two from an access control perspective.

5. Name at least 5 Logon Rights and 5 Privileges available in Microsoft GPOs.

6. Which privileges in a GPO can override permissions set on an object?

                                                   Current Version Date: 12/06/2010

7. What are the benefits of User Rights Assignments in your own words used as security controls and deployed across a domain of servers and workstations?

8. Explain why you would have to create a service account for applications and assign them elevated privileges with a GPO. Present a well thought out argument as to the danger, from the security perspective, in creating service accounts for applications and what can be done to mitigate the risk.

9. Provide at least 3 examples of either Rights or Privileges typically required by a service account in the User Rights Assignments section of a GPO.

10. Provide an explanation of why restricting access based on time zones or international users helps organizations achieve C-I-A as required by the Senate Chairs Group Policy Object definition? Assume Senate Chairs Group provides 24 x 7 x 365 customer service support in different time zones.

.

www.jblearning.com
Current Version Date: 12/06/2010

Laboratory #7

Lab #7: Design a Multi-factor Authentication Process

Learning Objectives and Outcomes

Upon completing this Lab, students will be able to complete the following tasks:

- Align appropriate authentication requirements to different data types per a defined data classification standard

- Define requirements for Remote Access from the Internet for the LAN-to-WAN Domain

- Align best practices for private sector and public sector authentication requirements that support online applications such as e-commerce, online banking, and online government

- Recommend best practices for remote access security measures and multi-factor authentication for employees and contractors through public Internet

- Assess and design proper authentication methods for RADIUS and TACACs+ authentication servers deployments as well as IEEE 802.11 WLAN infrastructures

Required Setup and Tools

This is a paper-based hands-on lab and does not require the use of the ISS "Mock" IT Infrastructure – Cisco core backbone network or VM server farm. Internet access and the student's Microsoft Office applications are needed to perform this hands-on paper-based lab.

The following summarizes the setup, configuration, and equipment needed to perform Lab #7:

1. Standard ITT ISS onsite student workstation must have the following software applications loaded and Internet access to perform this Lab:

   a. Microsoft Office 2007 or higher

   b. Adobe PDF Reader

Recommended Procedures

Hands-on Lab #7 – Student Steps:

Students should perform the following steps:

1. Browse to and open the FFIEC Authentication Guidance for Internet Banking:

   http://www.ffiec.gov/pdf/authentication_guidance.pdf

2. Investigate the following requirements for an Information Security Program:

   a. Identifies and assesses the risks associated with Internet-based products and services

Current Version Date: 12/06/2010

      b.   Identifies risk mitigation actions, including appropriate authentication strength

      c.   Measures and evaluates customer awareness efforts

3.   Investigate the following Recommended Risk Assessment Process:

      a.   Identify all transactions and levels of access associated with Internet-based customer products and services

      b.   Identify and assess the risk mitigation techniques, including authentication methodologies, employed for each transaction type and level of access

      c.   Include the ability to gauge the effectiveness of risk mitigation techniques for current and changing risk factors for each transaction type and level of access.

4.   Browse to the IASE/DISA STIGs website: http://iase.disa.mil/stigs/stig/index.html

5.   Download the following Secure Remote Computing Guideline Documents/ZIP File: unclassified_secure_remote_computing_v2r3_stig_20100827.zip

6.   Extract the.ZIP file and browse to the unzipped directory.

7.   Open the U_SRC_V2R3_Overview.pdf, this reviews the potential vulnerabilities and configuration recommendations for secure remote access as per DoD guidelines.

8.   Investigate the following concepts from this overarching DoD standards document for secure remote access:

      a.   Security Recommendations for Remote Access and Telework

      b.   Assessment, Enforcement and Remediation Services

      c.   Endpoint Security

      d.   Security Readiness Review Requirements

9.   Investigate the following Remote Access security checklist and guideline document on DoD requirements for Remote Access: U_Remote_Access_Policy_V2R3_STIG.pdf

      a.   Vulnerability Key: V0019834

          i.   Remote Privileged Access

10. Browse to and open the TACACs+ and RADIUS Comparison by Cisco Systems: http://www.cisco.com/application/pdf/paws/13838/10.pdf

11. Research and Compare TACACS+ and RADIUS in the following areas:

      a.   UDP and TCP

      b.   Packet Encryption

      c.   Authentication and Authorization

      d.   Multiprotocol Support

     e. Router Management

     f. Interoperability

     g. Traffic

     h. Device Support

Deliverables

Upon completion of Lab #7: Design a Multi-factor Authentication Process, the students are required to provide the following deliverables:

1. Lab #7 – Develop a chart listing the Remote Access Requirements of a financial On-line Banking facility and provide a written Multi-factor Authentication Plan explaining the implementation requirements and plan necessary.

2. Lab #7 – Lab Assessment Questions & Answers

Evaluation Criteria and Rubrics

The following are the evaluation criteria and rubrics for Lab #7 that the students must demonstrate:

1. Was the student able to align appropriate authentication requirements to different data types per a defined data classification standard? – [**20%**]

2. Was the student able to define the requirements for Remote Access from the Internet for the LAN-to-WAN Domain? – [**20%**]

3. Was the student able to align best practices for private sector and public sector authentication requirements that support online applications such as e-commerce, online banking, and online government? – [**20%**]

4. Was the student able to recommend best practices for remote access security measures and multi-factor authentication for employees and contractors through public Internet? – [**20%**]

5. Was the student able to assess and design proper authentication methods for RADIUS and TACACs+ authentication servers deployments as well as IEEE 802.11 WLAN infrastructures? – [**20%**]

                                 Current Version Date: 12/06/2010

Lab #7 – Assessment Worksheet

Design a Multi-factor Authentication Process

Course Name & Number: _____

Student Name: _____

Instructor Name: _____

Lab Due Date: _____

Overview

The students will research best practices for private sector and public sector authentication as it relates to e-commerce and on-line banking. Then they will research the best practices for remote access for employees through public Internet and for employees of city, county, state, and federal governments, based on DoD standards for secure remote access. Multi-factor authentication and restrictions based on data types and sensitivity as discussed in previous labs are major considerations for this research when investigating RADIUS, TACACs+ and WLAN authentication methodologies.

Lab Assessment Questions & Answers

1. In an Internet Banking Financial Institution is Single Factor Authentication acceptable? Why or why not?

2. Explain the difference between Positive Verification and Negative Verification?

3. What vulnerabilities are introduced by implementing a Remote Access Server?

4. What is a recommended best practice when implementing a Remote Access Policy server user authentication service?

5. Name at least 3 remote access protections or security controls that must be in place to provide secure remote access.

6. When dealing with RADIUS and TACACS+ for authentication methods, what protocols are used at Layer 4 for each of these techniques?

Current Version Date: 12/06/2010

7. In TACACS+ communications, what part of the packet gets encrypted and which part is clear text?

8. In RADIUS authentication, what is the purpose of the "Authenticator"?

9. Which of these two, RADIUS and TACACS+, combines both authentication and authorization?

10. Is combining authentication and authorization a less or more robust way of handling authentication? Explain.

Laboratory #8

Lab #8: Align Appropriate PKI Solutions Based on Remote Access and Data Sensitivity

Learning Objectives and Outcomes

Upon completing this lab, the students will be able to complete the following tasks:

- Identify solutions for remote access using PKI according to defined access controls and data classification standard requirements

- Design a layered remote access PKI solution that is based on the type of user and the type of data being accessed

- Compare and contrast PKI solutions for identification, authentication and authorization from security operations and management perspectives

- Identify the strengths and weaknesses within each type of encryption after a thorough comparison and analysis of pros and cons

- Align secure remote access protocols (IP-SEC, VPN, TLS, SSL, SSH, etc.) with different business application requirements and PKI capabilities

Required Setup and Tools

This is a paper-based hands-on lab and does not require the use of the ISS "Mock" IT Infrastructure – Cisco core backbone network or VM server farm. Internet access and the student's Microsoft Office applications are needed to perform this hands-on paper-based lab.

The following summarizes the setup, configuration, and equipment needed to perform Lab #8:

1. Standard ITT ISS onsite student workstation must have the following software applications loaded and Internet access to perform this Lab:

    a. Microsoft Office 2007 or higher

    b. Adobe PDF Reader

Recommended Procedures

Hands-on Lab #8 – Student Steps:

Students should perform the following steps:

1. Conduct research on the resources on the ITT Technical Institute Virtual Library on the following topics:

    a. Encryption

    b.   Public key infrastructure

    c.   Data privacy

    d.   Data security

2. Compare and contrast the two major classes of encryption and hashing

    a.   Symmetric

    b.   Asymmetric

    c.   Hash

3. Research the Primary Components of PKI Solutions

    a.   Certificate Authorities

    b.   Web of Trust

    c.   Temporary Certificates & Single Sign-On

    d.   Simple public key infrastructure

4. Compare Three Different Commercial PKI Solutions

    a.   Entrust http://www.entrust.com/

    b.   Public Key Infrastructure for Windows Server 2003 http://technet.microsoft.com/en-us/library/cc772670%28WS.10%29.aspx

    c.   RSA Certificate Manager http://www.rsa.com/node.aspx?id=1224

5. Investigate how PKI is leveraged with different protocols

    a.   VPNs and Public Key Infrastructure

        http://onlamp.com/pub/a/security/2004/09/23/vpns_and_pki.html

    b.   Deploying a Public Key Infrastructure with OpenSSL

        http://www.oreillynet.com/pub/a/security/2004/10/21/vpns_and_pki.html

    c.   Cisco Digital Certificates PKI for IPSec VPNs

        https://learningnetwork.cisco.com/servlet/JiveServlet/downloadBody/3592-102-1-9755/Digital%20Certificates%20PKI%20for%20IPSec%20VPNs.pdf

6. Research Private vs. Public Sector PKI Requirements to incorporate in written analysis

    a.   Federal Public Key Infrastructure Policy Authority

        http://www.idmanagement.gov/fpkipa/

    b.   NIST Public Key Infrastructures

        http://csrc.nist.gov/groups/ST/crypto_apps_infra/pki/index.html

    c.   PKI Policy Bodies and Other Authentication Frameworks http://www.oasis-pki.org/resources/policies/

Current Version Date: 12/06/2010

Deliverables

Upon completion of Lab #8: Align Appropriate PKI Solutions Based on Remote Access and Data Sensitivity, the students are required to provide the following deliverables:

1. Lab #8 – Develop a 3-5 page Summary of Findings report that discusses and highlights your research on Private vs. Public Sector PKI Requirements focusing on the following topics:

   a. The purpose, benefits, drawbacks, and methods of encryption identifying the major classification of encryption algorithms as symmetric, asymmetric or hashing.

   b. Data Classification and Sensitivity Considerations

   c. Incorporate digital signatures and block ciphers into the research summary

   d. Secure Remote Access Recommendations

2. Lab #8 – Assessment Worksheet with answers to the assessment questions

Evaluation Criteria and Rubrics

The following are the evaluation criteria and rubrics for Lab #8 that the students must perform:

1. Was the student able to identify solutions for remote access using PKI according to defined access controls and data classification standard requirements? – [**20%**]

2. Was the student able to align layered remote access PKI solutions based on the type of user and the type of data being accessed? – [**20%**]

3. Was the student able to compare and contrast PKI solutions for identification, authentication and authorization from security operations and management perspectives? – [**20%**]

4. Was the student able to identify the strengths and weaknesses within each type of encryption after a thorough comparison and analysis of pros and cons? – [**20%**]

5. Was the student able to align secure remote access protocols (IP-SEC, VPN, TLS, SSL, SSH, etc.) with different business application requirements and PKI capabilities? – [**20%**]

Current Version Date: 12/06/2010

Lab #8 – Assessment Worksheet

Align Appropriate PKI Solutions Based on Remote Access and Data Sensitivity

Course Name & Number: _____

Student Name: _____

Instructor Name: _____

Lab Due Date: _____

Overview

The student will research several PKI concepts and solutions that are based on the resources provided in the lab and the ITT library. He/she will discuss the role of PKI as it relates to remote access rights on classified data, based on the role of the user and the sensitivity of the data. The student will also review how to integrate PKI authentication into such technologies and protocols as IP-SEC, VPN, SSL and others, while taking into consideration both the private and public sector organizations. After creating the written analysis of encryption methods evaluating their benefits, roles and limitations, answer these assessment questions.

Lab Assessment Questions & Answers

1. Where can you store your public keys or public certificate files in the public domain? Is this the same thing as a Public Key Infrastructure (KI) server?

2. What do you need to do if you want to decrypt encrypted messages and files from a trusted sender?

3. When referring to IPSec Tunnel Mode, what two types of headers are available, and how do they differ?

4. Provide a step by step progression for a typical Certificate Enrollment process with a Certificate Authority.

5. When designing a PKI infrastructure what are the advantages and disadvantages of making the CA available publicly over the Internet or keeping it within the private network?

Current Version Date: 12/06/2010

6. Designing a PKI involves several steps. Per the Windows Best Practices for Designing a PKI, what are those steps? In your own words, explain what each step is meant to do.

7. When deploying a PKI, it is important to understand how many CAs will be necessary to properly implement the infrastructure. Provide 3-5 important considerations that must be taken into account before deploying a PKI for a large environment.

8. What is the main function of the certutil.exe command line tool available in Microsoft Windows?

9. What is the OpenSSL project and their mission?

10. What is the purpose of Single Sign-on? Provide one example of how it benefits security and one example as to how it can increase security risk.

Current Version Date: 12/06/2010

Laboratory #9

Lab #9: Apply Encryption to Mitigate Risk Exposure

Learning Objectives and Outcomes

Upon completing this lab, students will be able to complete the following tasks:

- Identify a Public Key Infrastructure (PKI) solution that can help ensure the confidentiality of business communications, and discuss the types of encryption in a summary to management

- Implement non-repudiation and the use of digital signatures when transmitting sensitive data over public and private networks

- Describe the role and the major components of a Certificate Authority (CA) in supporting an enterprise with a PKI environment and secure business communications

- Identify and compare shareware cryptography and encryption solutions to mitigate the risk from clear-text data and data transmissions

- Apply appropriate cryptography and encryption techniques for different data states and the type of protection available to protect each data state

Required Setup and Tools

This lab does not require the use of the ISS Mock IT Infrastructure - Cisco core backbone network. In addition, the Instructor VM workstation and Student VM workstations should be physically disconnected from the ITT internal network and be isolated on the classroom dedicated layer 2 switch. This will allow for a shared DHCP server to be used to allocate the IP addresses for the instructor and student workstations. The following components are required for this hands-on lab:

- A) A classroom workstation (with at least 2 Gig RAM) capable of supporting the removable hard drive with the VM server farm connected to the classroom layer 2 switch.

- B) An instructor workstation (with at least 4 Gig RAM recommended) that will act as the Instructor's demo lab workstation. The instructor will use the Instructor workstation's LCD projector to demo the loading and configuring of the Instructor VM workstation using VMware Player.

- C) Student Lab workstations will use their own VM server farm and VM student workstation. VMware Player will be used to run the Student VM and the Target VM.

Current Version Date: 12/06/2010

The following summarizes the setup, configuration, and equipment needed to perform Lab #9:

1. A Virtualized Server Farm with the following components:

    a. Microsoft DHCP server for allocating student IP host addresses

    b. A Student and/or Instructor VM

    c. A Windows 2003 Server VM (TargetWindows01)

2. Standard ITT ISS onsite student workstation must have the following software applications loaded to perform this Lab:

    a. VMware Player 3.x

    b. Microsoft Office 2007 or higher for Lab Assessment Questions & Answers

Recommended Procedures

Hands-on Lab #9 – Student Steps

Students should perform the following steps:

1. Connect your student-removable hard drive into a classroom workstation

2. Boot up the Student VM and "TargetWindows01" VM server within your workstation

3. Login to the Student VM and verify that GPG is pre-installed as an application.

4. Login to the "TargetWindows01" VM server as follows:

    ▪ Windows Server 2003 Standard Edition 32-bit (VM Name: "TargetWindows01")
       o Computer Name: Windows02
       o Three Users Available: administrator, instructor, or student (case sensitive)
       o Password: ISS316Security (case sensitive)
       o IP Address: DHCP
       o Domain Login: NO

5. On the Student VM, verify that GPG is pre-installed on the desktop. If not, check your \ITT_Tools\ folder on the hard drive for the GPG installation file

6. To open the program, click on GPG desktop program, and a prompt to create your private key will appear.

7. Insert the name PKIUser or <Your Name> as the name asked for. Click forward.

8. Insert an email, i.e. student@vlabs.com, and click forward.

9. Be sure that you create a backup copy of your new key when prompted, and click forward.

10. Enter a passphrase to further encrypt your newly created key.

Please write down this passphrase as it will be need to be used to decrypt and encrypt messages. (*password123* can be used as a passphrase for testing).

11. After generating the secret key, save it to the desktop to be able to easily find it later.

12. Click on close, and open up GPG again. Highlight the key you created, and click on the export option, and name the key PKIUser1 or <Your Name> as appropriate

13. Move over to the "TargetWindows01" VM server, and do the same, but use a different name like PKIUser2 or TargetWindows01

14. Transfer both sets of keys to each of the VMs using external HDD or a shared VM folder. Be sure that both public keys are on both VMs.

15. Use import button, and import keys to both VMs.

16. On Student VM, right click newly-imported key. Click on Set owner trust option, and set it to full in the options.

17. On the Student VM, right click the newly imported key, and click on the Sign keys option

18. Enter your secret key passphrase from earlier generation step to assign the public key to your secret keyring as "authorized".

19. Repeat steps 14 and 17 on the "TargetWindows01" VM server

20. For Hashing, we can verify the public key imported in each VM matches the Fingerprint in the GPG home window.

21. Now, on the Instructor VM, create a new file on the desktop using notepad. Name the file *encryptme.txt,* and add a message in the text file to your liking.

22. Once file is created and saved, you can right click and chose the sign and encrypt option.

23. Be sure you check the remove unencrypted file option at the bottom.

24. Add both certificates to the options, and click encrypt!

25. Once the file is encrypted, you will see it replace the plain text file on the desktop. Right click, and choose decrypt/verify option.

26. Now transfer the encrypted file to the "TargetWindows01" VM server desktop, and perform step 24 on the VM to decrypt the file on the other system.

27. Securing the file transfer with encrypted keys has now been successfully performed.

Deliverables

Upon completion of Lab #9: Apply Encryption to Mitigate Risk Exposure, the students are required to provide the following deliverables:

1. Lab #9 – Download shareware encryption software, and develop a demonstration to accompany the presentation on encryption. SEE: Lab #9 Supplemental Shareware Encryption Worksheet for shareware encryption resources.

2. Lab #9 – Lab Assessment Questions & Answers

Evaluation Criteria and Rubrics

The following are the evaluation criteria and rubrics for Lab #9 that the students must perform:

1. Was the student able to identify a Public Key Infrastructure (PKI) solution that can help ensure the confidentiality of business communications. Did he/she discuss the types of encryption in the summary to management? – [20%]

2. Was the student able to implement non-repudiation and the use of digital signatures when transmitting sensitive data over public and private networks? – [20%]

3. Was the student able to describe the role and the major components of a Certificate Authority (CA) in supporting an enterprise with a PKI environment and secure business communications? – [20%]

4. Was the student able to identify and compare shareware cryptography and encryption solutions to mitigate the risk from clear-text data and data transmissions? – [20%]

5. Was the student able to apply appropriate cryptography and encryption techniques for different data states and the type of protection available to protect each data state? – [20%]

 Current Version Date: 12/06/2010

Lab #9 – Supplemental Shareware Encryption Worksheet

Course Name & Number: _____

Student Name: _____

Instructor Name: _____

Lab Due Date: _____

Overview

For this lab task, the students will download and review various shareware versions of encryption tools from the Internet. The installation, the demonstration of its use, and the creation of public and private keys should be performed by each student..

Shareware Encryption Demonstration Requirements

1. Download and evaluate at least 3 shareware encryption tools from the Internet as provided below.

2. Security & Privacy / Encryption Tools – http://www.download32.com/encryption-tools-33033-category.html

3. TopShareware.com - http://www.topshareware.com/shareware-encryption-program/downloads/1.htm

4. Security & Encryption – http://www.ultrashareware.com/

5. USB Safeguard - 1.2.0 - http://www.download32.com/usb-safeguard-i83038.html

6. Cryptix - 0.85 - MAC OS - http://www.download32.com/cryptix-i83088.html

7. Advanced Encryption Package Professional 5.3.6 – http://www.download32.com/advanced-encryption-package-professional-i60038.html

8. Truecrypt - http://www.truecrypt.org/

9. Choose one of the three software tools evaluated and perform a demonstration in class of its uses.

                                    Current Version Date: 12/06/2010

Lab #9 – Assessment Worksheet

Apply Encryption to Mitigate Risk Exposure

Course Name & Number: _____

Student Name: _____

Instructor Name: _____

Lab Due Date: _____

Overview

The students will review the encryption mechanisms involved with implementing a PKI and the different methods of encryption needed to provide different functions within a PKI. They will also use GPG free encryption software to carry out digital signatures and secure communications. Hashing, symmetric encryption and asymmetric encryption are all covered during this hands-on demonstration. The students must now answer these s lab assessment questions.

Lab Assessment Questions & Answers

1. If you are using corporate e-mail for external communications that contain confidential information, what other security countermeasure can you employ to maximize the confidentiality of e-mail transmissions through the Internet?

2. Explain the role of a Certificate Authority and its obligations in authenticating the person or organization and issuing digital certificates.

3. What would a successful Subversion Attack of a CA result in?

4. What encryption mechanisms are built into Microsoft Windows XP Professional?

5. Could you add user's access to view your EFS encrypted files and folders? If so, how?

6. What would be needed by any Law Enforcement agency to decrypt encrypted messages easily?

7. What is SHA1, and what is it used for? Is it used similarly to TripleDES or are they different?

Current Version Date: 12/06/2010

8. Provide an explanation for the difference between symmetric keys and asymmetric keys in a PKI.

9. What is a common drawback to Encrypting using enterprise level tools?

10. Based on your research, submit your written assessment report of the three encryption tools you downloaded and tested. Explain what you like and dislike about the shareware encryption tools you reviewed.

Laboratory #10

Lab #10: Use Reconnaissance, Probing, & Scanning to Identify Servers and Hosts

Learning Objectives and Outcomes

Upon completing this lab, students will be able to complete the following tasks:

- Mitigate risk from unauthorized access to IT systems through proper testing and reporting port scanning and vulnerability scanning

- Develop a vulnerability scanning plan identifying potential access points throughout the seven domains of a typical IT infrastructure

- Implement tools to discover networks and operating systems, and conduct an IP host and OS discovery scan on a targeted server

- Recommend best practices to remediate weaknesses documented in the result of a vulnerability scan and determine enhancement requirements related to the type of data stored in the server

- Develop access control and security remediation plans for mitigating identified risks, threats, and vulnerabilities from the IP host and OS scans

Required Setup and Tools

This lab does not require the use of the ISS Mock IT Infrastructure - Cisco core backbone network. In addition, the Instructor VM workstation and Student VM workstations should be physically disconnected from the ITT internal network and be isolated on the classroom dedicated layer 2 switch. This will allow for a shared DHCP server to be used to allocate the IP addresses for the instructor and student workstations. The following is required for this hands-on lab:

A) A classroom workstation (with at least 2 Gig RAM) capable of supporting the removable hard drive with the VM server farm connected to the classroom layer 2 switch.

B) An instructor workstation (with at least 4 Gig RAM recommended) that will act as the Instructor's demo lab workstation. The instructor will display the Instructor workstation on the LCD projector to demo the loading and configuring of the Instructor VM workstation using VMware Player.

C) Student Lab workstations will use their own VM server farm and VM workstation. VMware Player will be used to run the Student VM and the Target VM.

Current Version Date: 12/06/2010

The following summarizes the setup, configuration, and equipment needed to perform Lab #10:

1. A Virtualized Server Farm with the following components:

    a. Microsoft DHCP server for allocating student IP host addresses

    b. A Student and/or Instructor XP VM

    c. A Windows 2003 Server VM (TargetWindows01)

2. Standard ITT ISS onsite student workstation must have the following software applications loaded to perform this Lab:

    a. VMware Player 3.x

    b. Microsoft Office 2007 or higher for Lab Assessment Questions & Answers

Nessus® v4.2.2 Vulnerability Assessment & Scanning Software

Training: Nessus® and Network Scanning Curriculums

If your information security teaching/training organization uses Nessus® in your curriculum to teach students how to scan for network vulnerabilities, the Tenable license allows you to use the HomeFeed subscription for your training purposes as can be found in Tenable's HomeFeed and ProfessionalFeed Subscription Agreement.

Program Rights, Requirements and Limitations:

You are permitted to copy/build images and redistribute Tenable's Nessus® and Tenable HomeFeed Plugins to students in and for the classroom setting only. Upon completion of the class, the ability to use the Plugins provided by the HomeFeed is terminated and students must re-register for either a HomeFeed or a ProfessionalFeed according to their intended use, as governed by the Subscription Agreement.

Information security organizations and students are not permitted to use the HomeFeed in a commercial fashion to secure their organization's or third party networks. It is only to be used for demonstration and teaching purposes in structured class environment.

 If you qualify for the right to use a Tenable subscription for your teaching/training organization, you are required to review the license agreement in its entirety.

Current Version Date: 12/06/2010

You will have the right and may use the Nessus® logo in your marketing of the class(es). If you choose to use the Nessus® logo, it must always be accompanied by the following: "Nessus® is a Registered Trademark of Tenable Network Security, Inc."

Tenable reserves the right to revoke a free subscription or terminate a subscription at its sole discretion at any time.

Nessus® Overview

Nessus® performs remote scans and audits of Unix, Windows, and network infrastructures. Nessus® can perform a network discovery of devices, operating systems, applications, databases, and services running on those devices.

Any non-compliant hosts running applications such as peer-to-peer, spyware or malware (worms, Trojans, etc.) are detected and identified. Nessus® is capable of scanning all ports on every device and issue remediation strategy suggestions as required.

Nessus® includes the ability to perform in-depth web application audits that identify vulnerabilities in custom built applications. Custom web applications can have their operating system, application, and SQL database audited and hardened against a variety of industry best practices and recommendations.

Recommended Procedures

Hands-on Lab #10 – Student Steps

Students should perform the following steps:

1. Perform unit reading and research the ITT Technical Institute Virtual Library on the following topics :
   a. Network Vulnerability Plan Development
   b. Network Vulnerability Scanning and Remediating
   c. Network Penetration Testing
   d. OS discovery
   e. Footprinting, Enumerating, etc....
2. Connect your student-removable hard drive into a classroom workstation
3. Power-up and log into the Student VM
4. Power-up and login to the "TargetWindows01" VM server as follows:

- - Windows Server 2003 Standard Edition 32-bit (VM Name: "TargetWindows01")
    - o Computer Name: Windows02
    - o Three Users Available: administrator, instructor, or student (case sensitive)
    - o Password: ISS316Security (case sensitive)
    - o IP Address: DHCP
    - o Domain Login: NO

5. Load ZeNmap GUI from the Student VM

6. Obtain the IP address of the "TargetWindows01" VM server by running ipconfig on said system

7. Enter the IP address of the "TargetWindows01" VM Server in the ZeNmap Target IP address field

8. Select "Intense Scan" from the drop-down menu

9. Click on start scan to perform the "Intense Scan"

10. Save your Nmap reconnaissance and probing scan report and submit this as part of your lab deliverables

11. Load the Nessus® v4.2.2.2 Server Manager in the Instructor VM

12. Connect to the Nessus® v4.2.2.2 Server Manager via an HTTPS:// secured browser connection as follows: https:// [server IP]:8834/ in the navigation bar

13. Login to the Nessus® Server Manager via your secure browser connection and authenticate

14. Prior to conducting a vulnerability scan, a policy definition is required and this is what will be demonstrated. A policy definition consists of the following configuration parameters for performing the vulnerability scan:

    a. Parameters that control technical aspects of the scan such as timeouts, number of hosts, type of port scanner and more.

    b. Credentials for local scans (e.g., Windows, SSH), authenticated Oracle Database scans, HTTP, FTP, POP, IMAP or Kerberos based authentication.

    c. Granular family or plug-in based scan specifications.

    d. Database compliance policy checks, report verbosity, service detection scan settings, UNIX compliance checks and more.

15. Once you have connected to a Nessus® server, you can create a custom policy by clicking on the "Policies" option on the bar at the top and then "+ Add" button on the right. The "Add Policy" screen will be displayed

16. Note that there are four configuration tabs: General, Credentials, Plug-ins and Preferences. For most environments, the default settings do not need to be modified, but they provide more granular control over the Nessus® scanner operation.

Current Version Date: 12/06/2010

a. General Tab – allows you to name your policy and define the scan related operations

b. Credentials Tab – The Credentials tab allows you to configure the Nessus® scanner to use authentication credentials during scanning. By configuring credentials, it allows Nessus® to perform a wider variety of checks that result in more accurate scan results.

c. Plug-Ins Tab - enables the user to choose specific security checks by plug-in family or individual checks

d. Preferences Tab - includes the means for granular control over scan settings. Selecting an item from the drop-down menu will display further configuration items for the selected category. Note that this is a dynamic list of configuration options that is dependent on the plug-in feed, audit policies and additional functionality that the connected Nessus® scanner has access to.

17. After creating a policy, you can create a new scan by clicking on the "Scans" option on the menu bar at the top and then click on the "+ Add" button on the right.

18. Performing an actual scan is not within scope of this Lab; however, if time permits run vulnerability scan on the "TargetWindows01" VM server can be performed.

19. Save and review the scan results from your ZenGUI Nmap scan, and answer the lab assessment questions

Deliverables

Upon completion of Lab #10: Use Reconnaissance, Probing, & Scanning to Identify Servers and Hosts, students are required to provide the following deliverables:

1. Lab #10 – Reconnaissance & Probing Scan Report – Results of the ZenGUI Nmap scan with an accompanying executive summary

2. Lab #10 – Lab Assessment Questions & Answers

Current Version Date: 12/06/2010

Evaluation Criteria and Rubrics

The following are the evaluation criteria and rubrics for Lab #10 that the students must perform:

1. Was the student able to mitigate risk from unauthorized access to IT systems through proper testing and reporting port scanning and vulnerability scanning? – **[20%]**

2. Was the student able to develop a vulnerability scanning plan identifying potential access points throughout the seven domains of a typical IT infrastructure? – **[20%]**

3. Was the student able to implement tools to discover networks and operating systems, and conduct an IP host and OS discovery scan on a targeted server? – **[20%]**

4. Was the student able to recommend best practices to remediate weaknesses documented in the result of a vulnerability scan and determine the enhancement requirements related to the type of data stored in the server? – **[20%]**

5. Was the student able to develop access control and security remediation plans for mitigating identified risks, threats, and vulnerabilities from the IP host and OS scans? – **[20%]**

Current Version Date: 12/06/2010

Lab #10 – Assessment Worksheet

Use Reconnaissance, Probing, & Scanning to Identify Servers and Hosts

Course Name & Number: _____

Student Name: _____

Instructor Name: _____

Lab Due Date: _____

Overview

The students will perform OS fingerprinting and Vulnerability Scanning using Nmap and Nessus®. They will also review general network scanning and reconnaissance tools and be able to explain the differences between vulnerability scanning and penetration testing. Answer the following assessment questions.

Lab Assessment Questions & Answers

1. Describe what ZenMap GUI performs to do passive OS fingerprinting?

2. Nmap can also help define applications that are available on the machines it is scanning. How does it know the application? Is this a reliable method of identifying running services on a target machine?

3. Why would you want to use Nmap before an attack as opposed to after the attack?

4. How does Nessus® differ from Nmap (ZeNmap GUI) and which tool would you use for network discovery and inventory versus identifying software vulnerabilities?

5. What is the purpose of defining a Policy definition as a first step in performing a Nessus® vulnerability scan?

6. Name the five things you can configure as part of a vulnerability scan in Nessus®?

7. Will Nessus® provide a security practitioner any information regarding remediating vulnerability found while doing the vulnerability scanning?

Current Version Date: 12/06/2010

8. What is the major difference between a penetration test and a vulnerability assessment? In your opinion, should an organization perform both or does one or the other meet all the needs for most?

9. What are the criteria by which PCI Compliance Audits determine whether your organization needs to perform periodic vulnerability scans or not? How often should you scan?

10. The students are to save their "Intense Scan" on "TargetWindows01" VM server using ZenGUI Nmap and submit the scan report along with an executive summary, summarizing the findings, assessment, and recommendations that the student has to mitigate any identified risks, threats, or vulnerabilities.

Current Version Date: 12/06/2010